Extreme

SKY-DIVING

Virginia Loh-Hagan

⊙45th Parallel Press

Published in the United States of America by Cherry Lake Publishing
Ann Arbor, Michigan
www.cherrylakepublishing.com

Content Adviser: Liv Williams, Editor, www.iLivExtreme.com
Reading Adviser: Marla Conn, ReadAbility, Inc.
Photo Credits: ©Germanskydiver/Shutterstock.com, cover, 1; ©Buzz Pictures/Alamy, 5; ©Danshutter/Shutterstock.com, 6; ©Germanskydiver/Dreamstime.com, 8; ©Habman_18/istockphoto.com, 11; ©Anna Yakimova/Dreamstime.com, 13; ©Taufoto/Dreamstime.com, 14; ©Archivist/Alamy, 17; ©Jeff Schultes/Dreamstime.com, 19; ©Rick Neves/Shutterstock.com, 21; ©Digital Vision/Thinkstock.com, 23; ©Europics/Newscom, 25; ©Luke Aikins/ZUMApress/Newscom, 27; ©Germanskydiver/Shutterstock.com, 29; ©Trusjom/Shutterstock.com, multiple interior pages; ©Kues/Shutterstock.com, multiple interior pages

45th Parallel Press is an imprint of Cherry Lake Publishing.

Library of Congress Cataloging-in-Publication Data

Loh-Hagan, Virginia.
  Extreme skydiving / Virginia Loh-Hagan.
    pages cm. -- (Nailed It!)
  Includes bibliographical references and index.
  ISBN 978-1-63470-021-4 (hardcover) -- ISBN 978-1-63470-075-7 (pdf) -- ISBN 978-1-63470-048-1 (paperback) -- ISBN 978-1-63470-102-0 (ebook)
  1. Skydiving--Juvenile literature. 2. Extreme sports--Juvenile literature. 3. ESPN X-Games--Juvenile literature. I. Title. II. Title: Extreme skydiving.

GV770.L65 2015
797.5′6--dc23

                    2015006291

ABOUT THE AUTHOR

Dr. Virginia Loh-Hagan is an author, university professor, former classroom teacher, and curriculum designer. She likes to ride in planes, not jump out of them. She lives in San Diego with her very tall husband and very naughty dogs. To learn more about her, visit www.virginialoh.com.

Table of Contents

Humans Can Fly!

What is extreme skydiving? What are the different types of extreme skydiving?

It's a bird! It's a plane! It's a **UFO**!

People looked up at the night sky. They saw strange, bright lights. Many reported an **unidentified** flying object, or UFO. Unidentified means they don't know what it is. People thought they saw an alien ship.

Jon DeVore and Sean MacCormac are not aliens. They are skydivers. They skydived at night. They used **flares**. Flares make bright lights. That's what people saw!

Jay Stokes also loves skydiving. He set a record for most jumps in a day. He did 640 jumps. He jumped about every two minutes. He used three airplanes. They took him back into the sky. He wants to do 700 skydives in a day.

Skydiving can feel like flying.

Skydivers jump from planes. They jump from 16,000 feet (4,877 meters) above the ground. They **free-fall**. They fly in the air for a while. Skydiving doesn't feel like falling. It feels like floating or flying.

Parachute is a French word. It translates to "prevent fall."

Spotlight Biography: Krish Shanghvi

In 2012, Krish Shanghvi became the world's youngest skydiver. He was 8 years old. He is from Mumbai, India. He jumped from a plane. He was 10,000 feet (3,048 m) above the ground. He did a free fall for 45 seconds. Then he opened his parachute. In India, skydivers need to be at least 16 years old. So he had to go South Africa to skydive. Krish has an older brother. His name is Parth. Parth set a record as the youngest scuba diver. He did this in February 2010, when Krish was 6 years old. Krish wanted to copy his big brother and set a record. And he did!

Skydivers open a **parachute**. A parachute looks like a balloon top. It slows skydivers as they land. They steer the parachute. They land in special places called **drop zones**.

Some extreme skydivers jump from higher **altitudes**, or heights. These skydivers jump from 30,000 feet (9,144 m).

In formation skydiving, skydivers can make patterns in the air.

They need oxygen masks and tanks. There are two types of these jumps. HALO is one type. HALO means a High Altitude Low Opening jump. Skydivers free-fall for several minutes. They open their parachutes at the last minute. The military developed HALO. They didn't want soliders to be seen by enemies.

HAHO is the second type. HAHO means a High Altitude High Opening jump. Skydivers open their parachutes soon after jumping. They glide before landing.

There are other types of extreme skydiving. **Formation** skydiving is also called belly-flying. Skydivers' bellies face down to earth. Skydivers create formations in free fall. Formations are when skydivers join in the air. Skydivers hold each other's arms or legs. There can be two or more skydivers. Sometimes they do tricks.

Nearly 140 skydivers jumped from 18,500 feet (5,639 m) above ground. They flew upside down. They linked arms and legs. They made a huge snowflake! It was 160 feet

(48.8 m) wide. This was hard to do. They tried 15 times. They tried over three days. Skydivers came from all around the world. They finally did it!

Free-flying is when skydivers do tricks in the air. They stand up. They fly upside down. They fly over each other. They fly under each other. They fly around each other. They also make formations.

Freestyle skydiving is like **ballet**. Skydivers dance in free fall. They do loops and spins.

Skydivers also like to **swoop**. They swoop through the air. "Swoopers" jump from lower in the sky. They jump from 5,000 feet (1,524 m). They open their parachutes quickly. They fly at high speed. They fly low to the ground before landing. Flying low makes it dangerous. Shannon Pilcher said, "To travel this fast, this close to the ground ... it feels amazing." Jessica Edgeington said, "There's nothing like it. It's the closest thing to human flight."

Swooping is sometimes called canopy piloting.

Dangers of Skydiving!

Why is extreme skydiving dangerous? How can extreme skydivers get hurt?

It's important for skydivers to have the correct gear. They must carry two parachutes. One is the main parachute. If there is a problem, they use the other parachute. It's called the **reserve**. Reserve means it's extra or a backup.

Skydiving is thrilling. It's also dangerous. Craig Stapleton had done 7,000 skydives. He was doing a hard stunt. His parachutes failed. He spun through the air. He crash-landed. He was not hurt.

One time, the engine of a skydiving plane failed. It crashed into a lake. Thirteen skydivers jumped from the plane before it crashed. None of them were hurt. But it was scary.

Skydivers get hurt for different reasons. Some skydivers do unsafe things. They do stunts before they're ready. Some

Skydivers sometimes don't land where they want to.

Skydivers need to check their gear.

make mistakes. They don't steer correctly. They don't pack their gear right. Changing winds affect landing speed. This means skydivers can't control their parachutes. Sometimes, parachutes hit each other.

Skydiving from high places is dangerous. Planes can crash. Skydivers can also get sick from being so high. They lose oxygen.

Extreme Skydiving: Know the Lingo

Arch: a skydiving position

Canopy: the umbrella part of the parachute

Climbout: being mostly outside the plane door and getting ready to jump

Cork: losing control and falling quickly

Dock: making contact with another skydiver in free fall

Drogue: a smaller parachute to slow down falling

Hook turn: a steep dive

Jump run: the flight of the airplane

Opening point: the moment when a skydiver opens the parachute

Pack: preparing a parachute system before jumping

Relative work: when two or more people meet in midair

Rig: the parachute system

Ripcord: a metal cable that opens the parachute

Water jump: landing in water

Whuffo: someone who is not a skydiver

Inventing Wings

What is ballooning? What did early skydivers do?
How did the military develop skydiving? What is a wingsuit?

Flying machines were invented long ago. **Daredevils** wanted to fly, too. Daredevils are people who take risks.

Ballooning was a popular activity. People rode in hot-air balloons. Daredevils jumped out of them. In 1797, André-Jacques Garnerin jumped from a balloon. He was strapped to a big parachute. He did stunts in the air. He did this all over Europe.

Airplanes first flew in 1903. Daredevils were jumping out of them in no time. Leslie Irvin did the first free fall in 1919. He did stunts for movies. He proved that skydivers could be in control when the parachute opened. In 1925, Steven Budreau was the first to do a long free fall. He stopped his body from spinning. He moved his arms and legs. Early skydivers had to figure out their sport.

Skydiving changed from jumping out of hot-air balloons to jumping out of airplanes.

Early skydivers performed in shows. They jumped from old, shaky planes. They did loops and other tricks. They walked on the airplane's wings. This was called **barnstorming**. It was like a flying circus.

Georgia "Tiny" Broadwick was a popular barnstormer. She was the first woman to jump from a plane. She was

Getting Your Body Ready

High-altitude jumping is dangerous. There is a change in air pressure. Ears pop. Ears try to balance the pressure. People breathe less oxygen. This means they breathe faster. Being high in the sky can cause confusion. It can also cause paralysis. Paralysis means not being able to move body parts. Skydivers prepare to be in high altitudes. Adrian Nicholas would breathe pure oxygen before going high in the air. He did this for an hour. This helped him avoid altitude sickness. Other skydivers train their heart and lungs. They run, walk, and swim.

The Golden Knights is the U.S. Army's skydiving team.

also the first woman to do a free fall. She broke bones. She hurt her shoulder. She landed in swamps. She was dragged by her parachute. She jumped from a burning balloon. She said, "I was never afraid. I'd go up any time, any place. The only thing I hated was getting back to earth so quickly."

The military also developed skydiving. It saved the lives of airplane crews. It was also a way to deliver soldiers to the battlefield.

Adrian Nicholas invented wings for humans. His **wingsuit** was a one-piece outfit. It had webbing between the legs and arms. Air filled the wingsuit to create wings. The wingsuit lifted his body.

Nicholas tested his wingsuit in an air tunnel. Then he tested it when he jumped from airplanes. He had to get used to the thin air. He was 36,000 feet (10,973 meters) above land. The airplane door opened. He jumped out. He plunged to Earth. He flew in his wingsuit for as long as possible. He opened his parachute. His oxygen mask froze. He kept improving his wingsuit.

Some skydivers like to wear wingsuits. They look like flying squirrels. They fall more slowly than skydivers in a free fall. This means they get to fly longer. They still need a parachute. They need to slow down before landing.

"Some skydivers like to wear wingsuits. They look like flying squirrels."

Wingsuits let skydivers get more time in free fall.

Flying to the Next Level

What is pyrotechnic skydiving? What is skysurfing?
What is wingboarding? What is a Paratrooper?

Skydivers are always coming up with new ideas. There is a professional skydiving team in Ohio. They practice **pyrotechnic** skydiving. Pyrotechnics are fireworks. This team sets off fireworks as they jump from planes. Fireworks are strapped to their legs. They burn fireworks while they join arms in a free fall. Then they carefully open their parachutes. They avoid the flames. They don't want to burn themselves. John Hart is the team leader. He said, "It's pretty cool how we can actually create fireworks shows as we jump."

Skydivers created skysurfing. They wear a board attached to their feet. They do surfing tricks. They do loops, rolls, and spins during the free fall. Skysurfing is dangerous. The board could fall. That would hurt people on the ground.

Aaron Wypyszynski wants to create a new sport. He wants to combine wakeboarding, skydiving, and wingsuit flying.

The skysurfing boards are about the size of snowboards.

When Extreme Is Too Extreme!

Anthony Martin handcuffed his hands to a belt around his waist. His right arm was chained to the inside of a coffin. He locked himself in the coffin. He used a prison door lock. There was no key. Two skydivers held the handles of the coffin and jumped out of a plane. They were 14,500 feet (4,419 m) above ground. They were in free fall. The coffin moved a lot. Martin picked the lock. He struggled to open the door. He escaped! He somersaulted out of the coffin. He opened his parachute. He landed safely. Martin is an escape artist. He was inspired by famous magician Harry Houdini. This was the second time Martin had tried this trick. He has only skydived 17 times. He works on not being scared. He said, "Fear is one of those emotions that kind of distracts from your ability to think clearly and be effective."

Skydivers combine sports to make skydiving more exciting.

He calls it wingboarding. A wingboard is a board with wings. A plane tows, or pulls, a wingboarder. Wypyszynski was inspired by a Disney TV show called *TaleSpin*. A character surfs on a cloud. He rides a metal board. He is towed by a plane.

Another invention is the **Paratrooper**. This is a folding bike. It is made for jumping out of planes. The military developed it. They wanted to drop soldiers into battle. The bike has 27 speeds. It folds in 20 seconds. New inventions allow skydivers to dream of new sports.

Imagining the Impossible

What is space-diving? Who is Felix Baumgartner?
Who is Alan Eustace?

Space-diving could be the future's most extreme sport. Orbital Outfitters is a company that creates a special space suit. It will let humans jump to Earth from outer space. Skydivers would jump from a rocket ship. They'll be 60 miles (96.5 kilometers) above Earth. This is 10 times higher than planes can fly. This space suit could also help **astronauts**. Astronauts travel to space. Sometimes space missions go wrong. The suit would let them return safely to Earth.

Felix Baumgartner tested such a suit. He jumped from a special balloon. It had a small spaceship underneath it. He jumped from 23 miles (37 km) above Earth. He tumbled in the free fall. But he saved himself. This was the longest and highest free fall. Space is the next step. Space is only 37 miles (59.5 km) more away.

In October 2014, Alan Eustace did a **stratosphere** jump. The stratosphere is a layer in Earth's atmosphere. Eustace jumped from a balloon that was 26 miles (41.8 km) above Earth. He wore a special suit and could breathe pure oxygen. His free fall lasted four and a half minutes. He traveled at 822 miles (1,323 km) per hour. He broke the

Felix Baumgartner set records for high-altitude skydives. He set records for speeds in free fall.

Advice from the Field: Use Hand Signals

Skydivers have to respect each other. They avoid being on top of other skydivers. They don't want to fall into someone else's parachute. They give a wave-off signal before opening their parachutes. They make sure everyone is away from them. Skydivers have other hand signals. Some students get nervous when they're free-falling. Skydiving instructors pat the top of their students' heads. This means to stay calm. Daniel Pharr survived a very scary skydive. His instructor had a heart attack. They were in the air. Daniel said, "Assess the situation and keep a calm head about you, because it doesn't do any good to panic."

sound barrier. This is where a speeding object passes the speed of sound. It took him 15 minutes to land. He set a record for the highest free fall jump. He also set a record for total free fall distance.

Balloons, planes, rocket ships—what will skydivers jump out of next?

Can you believe skydivers want to jump from space? There are no limits for skydivers.

Did You Know?

- The military trains dogs to skydive. They jump with an officer. Dogs are trained to smell hidden bombs. They are also trained to find victims of plane crashes. Dogs travel with cameras to send pictures back to the military. Hooch is the only dog to skydive and scuba dive. She had to quit when she fell out of bed and broke her leg.

- Leonardo da Vinci was the first person to think of a parachute. He drew a picture of a parachute in 1495. He dreamed of humans being able to fly. He designed gliders.

- Roberta Mancino is a former model. She skydives wearing high heels.

- Flying squirrels have flaps of skin like a wingsuit. This is how they fly from tree to tree. Skydivers wearing wingsuits look like flying squirrels.

- Former President George H. W. Bush skydived for his 85th and 90th birthdays.

- Daredevil Rob Bradley used to teach math. He used his skydives to teach kids about speed, distance, and time. "I would actually plot graphs of my skydives, then use them to make calculations," he said.

- People have done some strange things while skydiving. One person got a tattoo while in a free fall. Another got a haircut.

Consider This!

TAKE A POSITION! Many professional athletes have contracts. They are not allowed to do extreme sports like skydiving. Their teams are afraid they'll get hurt. These athletes can't put their body at risk. They need to be able to play their sports. If they skydive, they could get in trouble. Do you think this is fair? What do you think about this issue? Argue your point with reasons and evidence.

SAY WHAT? Learn more about BASE jumping. BASE jumping also involves jumping from high places. How are BASE jumping and skydiving similar? How are they are different?

THINK ABOUT IT! "Full contact skydiving" combines skydiving and martial arts. It's like fighting in the air. Some people thought this was a real sport. But it was a joke. No one actually does it. Create a new skydiving sport. What would you call it? What would be some of the moves?

SEE A DIFFERENT SIDE! Skydivers jump because they like the feeling of being free. They like the excitement of doing something dangerous. Learn more about the dangers of skydiving. Do you think the dangers are greater than the rewards?

Learn More: Resources

Primary Sources

Where the Sun Always Shines, a documentary about skydiving (directed by Emilio Mamuyac): www.wherethesunalwaysshinesmovie.com

Secondary Sources

Gigliotti, Jim. *Skydiving.* Mankato, MN: Child's World, 2012.

McFee, Shane. *Skydiving.* New York: PowerKids, 2008.

Niver, Heather Moore. *Skydiving.* New York: Gareth Stevens Publishing, 2014.

Web Sites

National Skydiving League: ww1.skyleague.com

Red Bull Air Force: http://redbullairforce.com

United States Parachute Association: www.uspa.org

Glossary

altitudes (AL-tih-toodz) high heights

astronauts (AS-truh-nawts) space pilots

ballet (ba-LAY) graceful dance

barnstorming (BARN-storm-ing) a flying circus, with tricks done in the air and on the plane

daredevils (DAIR-dev-uhlz) risk takers

drop zones (DRAHP ZOHNZ) designated places to land

flares (FLAYRZ) devices that make bright lights

formation (for-MAY-shuhn) skydivers joining in the air to form a shape

free-fall (FREE-fawl) to fly in the air for a while after jumping and before landing

parachute (PA-ruh-shoot) a piece of strong, light fabric attached to thin ropes that helps skydivers slow down their fall through the air

Paratrooper (PA-ruh-troop-ur) a type of folding bike

pyrotechnic (py-roh-TEK-nik) involving fire or fireworks

reserve (rih-ZURV) extra, backup

sound barrier (SOUND BEYR-ee-ur) point where a speeding object passes the speed of sound

stratosphere (STRAT-uh-sfeer) a layer in Earth's atmosphere

swoop (SWOOP) to sweep through the air

UFO (YOO-EFF-OH) stands for unidentified flying object

unidentified (uhn-eye-DEN-tuh-fide) unable to figure out

wingsuit (WING-soot) a one-piece outfit with webbing between the legs and arms

Index